A MODERN DAY SCREWTAPE LETTERS

TANNER LAUZON

ACKNOWLEDGEMENT

I want to thank a few people who specifically helped me on this project and took time to either help with editorial work, and graphics, or solely were friends who encouraged me throughout the writing process. First, a would like to thank *lauren thomas* who created the cover art and spent countless hours making it look exactly how i asked. she was so willing to help and sacrifice her own time to do so. i would also like to thank *annalise ousley* for all the editorial work she put into this book. she spent an immense amount of time sitting with me giving me the greatest suggestions and helping with simple grammatical errors i missed. she also was so encouraging as she edited the book leaving notes that inspired me to continue writing. i would also like to thank my friends *emma thomas, caleb krieg,* and *cole stark.* when i first announced i was releasing this book they were in many ways more ecstatic about it than i was. throughout the months of the writing process, they encouraged me in numerous ways and continually checked in with the book's progress. finally, i would like to thank *you.* it is a dream of mine to become a full-time writer and the support you show just by reading this, leaving a review, or whatever you do has and will continue to impact me for the rest of my life. i truly will never be able to thank you guys enough.

A MODERN DAY SCREWTAPE LETTERS

PURPOSE

before the start of the book, i want to express why i started writing and how i came to love it. i grew up controlled by my mind, continually lost in thoughts that did not seem like my own. because of this it became my prison yet my comfort. hopelessness and defeat was my entity. at the age of 18, this all changed. i encountered Jesus and His love for the first time. i grew up as an angry agnostic who wanted to believe in a God but thought He hated me because of all of the tragedies i faced starting at a young age. once i experienced the True Love of God my life changed forever. i would love to give you a happy ever after story but that will not be the case quite yet. Jesus changed my life, but this does not mean there was not still a constant war going on within my mind. rather, i learned how to deal with it with the Father. i believe in full healing and that Jesus can heal right away but i also believe in a Father who loves to hold His son in his hurting. that is exactly what God did. i realized i now served the most Creative being in the universe so that also meant i got to ask Him what to create. He showed me that writing would be a way to help my thoughts while also a way to get to know God more and even get to know myself more in the midst of it all. it was as if the Hand of God would take my pen and write my thoughts on paper for me. the God of the universe wants this same type of relationship with you. Jesus who is God, came down from Heaven to die for you paying your debt. He did this so we could have a relationship with Him for eternity. perhaps it was so i could write Him love letters for eternity. i have two questions for you. 1. if you have never accepted Jesus into your heart will you do that today? 2. if you have accepted Him into your heart, how can you make your relationship with Him personal and how do you or can you allow Him to pour out His love through you?

CONTENTS

PREFACE:

CHAPTER 1: the Light

CHAPTER 2: a new light

CHAPTER 3: controlling the new light

CHAPTER 4: within the new light

CHAPTER 5: mirror mirror

CHAPTER 6: a ball of clay

CHAPTER 7: eternity on earth

CHAPTER 8: desires of the heart

CHAPTER 9: a cloud of deceit

CHAPTER 10: fear, futile, and future

CHAPTER 11: lights against Light

CONTENTS

CHAPTER 12: what is Love?

CHAPTER 13: work to death

CHAPTER 14: fleeting fame

CHAPTER 15: numb and broken

CHAPTER 16: seeing the Light

CHAPTER 17: following the Light

CHAPTER 18: a cry for identity

CONCLUDING THOUGHTS

A MODERN DAY
SCREWTAPE LETTERS

PREFACE

in my opinion, the beauty of humanity is thought and reasoning. we as a society ration to navigate through the complexities of the realm, we live in. we strive to find utmost truth and understanding of the existence of all things. this book is not only for those who believe in the deity of Christ, rather it is for anyone who loves deep thought and desires to think in a way many have never before. as a lover of thought, understanding, and philosophy this book engages the mind to surpass understanding and take a deeper look at the universe. the dialogue that happens within this book is a narration between three characters. two demons consult on how to torment their patient (a human). one advises the other on different strategies and tactics of how to keep the patient from seeing the Light, the Love of Jesus, or Truth. a goal of mine is to divulge problematic philosophical concerns in today's society and encourage the reader to discover Absolute Truth for himself. if Truth is real then there must be masses of false things that strive to act as Truth. subjective Truth is not Truth at all then it is relative. if we do not have any absolute and eternal truth then everything is relative, and relativity leads to chaos.

    with that being said, i want to form a foundation prior to the start of this book. the devil is a misleader and so are the demons that run with him. i do not mean for this to instill fear in any manner; rather this means precautions are necessary. that is the thesis of my writing; to show you the intricacy and the depth devils may use to come against us. more importantly, how much more powerful the ways of Christ and His thoughts are. the world is full of darkness and i am writing to you to expose it. i want to show you that the Light, Christ Jesus Himself, will always prevail. even before i found myself in Christianity i knew these things were real. i watched as i allowed them to play and torment my mind for years. they had full control over me and did as they pleased. when you are fully immersed in darkness it is a cloud that blocks you from seeing the Light. the soldiers of darkness recruit you and make war the only thing you know. however, the battle has already been won. this is why devils fixate on the battle and cultivate a war within. furthermore, Light can and will prevail through the fog of darkness. all why you, my friend, need to *act* like Light. our patient mustn't take one glance into the Light or we may lose him entirely. the first thing i want to consult you on my dear friend is our patient's *sight*. friend, we mustn't allow him to use his eyes for their intended purpose. tell him that he is seeing when he is fully blind, and he may never notice he has not been seeing all along. allow him to think his thoughts are sight. the patient is meant to see and see clearly for that matter. perhaps we can allow him to see if his eyes are not seeing rightly. which in the end, means he would not be seeing at all. the perspective would then be ours and not the Light's. those who do not know the Light can be deceived of anything being the Light. so, this is our main goal. keep the patient away from even a partial view of the Light because even in part, the Light shines fully and reveals unending waves of peace separating our patient from us forevermore. have the patient's head not even face the direction Light may come from. let his mind be a chessboard. play around until you find the right moves to sustain your patient in darkness. infiltrate with urgency and know this, my friend, somehow and someway the Light can still shine amid the darkness. He comes like a thief in the night, stealing our patients and bringing them into His covenant of Light. the Light is unpredictable and in doing so is very irritable. i urge you friend, keep the patient's sight on darkness and darkness alone. let them reside with us forevermore.

YOUR BELOVED OLDER BROTHER,
HAVOC

CHAPTER 2
a new light
*the start of a new era of
social media & technology*

dear mr. sagewort,

    my friend, i have good news to bear. it has been quite some time yet i have stumbled upon a new discovery that may pertain to your efforts with your patient. i have discovered a new *light* source that is a steeple to the mind. it will enclose a patient in their own thoughts furthermore. enchanting one in *their* knowledge of a light rather than The Light Itself. this new light allows any patient who has access to it to gain any portion of knowledge and bring forth any notion *their* mind may desire. yes, any notion a patient may desire. it is a way to dwindle sight on Light and give the patient a whole new view of what Light really is. let me explain my dear friend. we will be able to tell a sick patient he is healthy, and he will believe it. this is medicine that causes the soul to become numb to the agony it goes through. i have observed as they take medicine to stop the body from feeling pain; why would we not use knowledge to do the same to the soul? the darkened abyss called the soul becomes a bliss to the vagabond mind because the patient is now fixated on other matters. i tell you once again a sick patient will believe he is healthy. marvelous, isn't it?

<mark>our job becomes easy when all he thinks about is himself.</mark> this makes me snicker because we from the outside know he is not thinking of himself at

all; it is just a matrix within his soul in which he fully believes is himself. so, with urgency, i tell you, you mustn't withhold this from your patient. allow him to believe this temporal knowledge and as much of it as he may please. i adore seeing how a bedridden patient may think he is healthy and back to the normality of their life while being kept in the hand of our king forevermore.

    the new light allows for knowledge without the Source. it is a river without a mountain top. a river always starts upstream. creating an artificial source to the flowing river. the source is not real whatsoever. healing will happen without the patient actually being Healed. it is more of a temporary aid that acts as an eternal home. let your patient explore the fascinations of this new light; allowing them to fall deep into the forest of darkness. the new light becomes the source for our patient. yes, at some point it can be the knowledge and a source. no longer will he have a necessity to sit and wait for the Light to be revealed to them; rather, the new light draws our patient in like a fish on a hook waiting for another bite. he thinks he will be fed while in the end he will perish and be eaten by his own flesh. give this new light to any patient and they may just never even think to question The Light's validity ever again. The Light will become mere ashes rather than the Radiating Beam It truly is. knowledge is an antidote for the soul but if mixed properly becomes venom in the mind. we must use it as a cloak over the wounded soul.

YOUR BELOVED OLDER BROTHER,

HAVOC

CHAPTER 3

controlling the new light

dear mr. sagewort,

i have been observing the patient and noticed some places where you are at fault. you have been quite foolish for allowing the patient to occupy his time with other patients rather than having him look at this new light i told you about a few months ago. the depth of trust your patient has with those around him is concerning. it almost seems as if you do not care about the mission set before you. would you like me to take over or do you think you have it in you to torment day and night? if not, i will gladly find 70 other brothers to do the deed for you just so i know the patient stays within our grasp. let me give you a few more details about this patient in particular so you may understand my heart and why i am so aggravated that this is occurring. our patient feels the filthy thing called *love* while with those he is closest to. he trusts because that is something that is written on every patient's heart. however, when he trusts, it brings him out of the cloud of deceit and into residence of joy. disgusting, is it not? an utter abomination to the craft i have spent countless times trying to teach you, my dear friend. communal relations is the last thing i desire this patient to have because every time he is in this setting somehow, someway, the Light reveals Himself to our puny patient. i am unwell by this and unsure how it is possible. i have just now come to the conclusion that this is reality for him. i urge you to prevent him from this! this aggravates our king immensely and it is not good if he is aggravated with me. so, i urge you once more to use this new light as a form of separation. we in the darkness know that Light separates darkness from darkness so allow this new light to be a fortress between him and those around him. i am unsure of how to hinder him from having these conversations. all i know is that implementing this light in front of his eyes is crucial. your patient longs for communal time so perhaps there may be a way for the patient to believe this new light provides that comfort to his spirit. i must take time to process the unfortunate things you have allowed your patient to do and will get back to you in due time.

YOUR BELOVED OLDER BROTHER,

HAVOC

CHAPTER 4

within the new light

eight years later…

dear mr. sagewort,

    my dear friend, i write to you expectant of victory. i have found a way to not only bring our patients to the new light but put the patient within the new light. this is radiation to the mind. static that will fill every waking thought within our patients' minds. so i urge you **proceed with caution*.* i have realized quickly many facets will draw them near to this new light. furthermore, it is now possible to be drawn *into* this new light. i have seen tactics that do this but i have yet to see it to this extent. in the past i have been the commander and my patients were my soldiers. i fed them what they needed to fight in a war i know they have already lost. i am an enemy who has infiltrated as their commander. now you have placed your patient into the battlefield and all we must do is let it be and watch as he is fully submerged in a sea of thoughts. this is exciting. we can simply pass control to the new light he scrolls on, and it becomes his commander. we can sit like kings and feast on the depravity of his soul as the new commander guides him to deconstruction. the patient is enticed to think as he scrolls, he consumes everything while the phenomenon is quite the opposite. his mind consumes an exorbitant amount at the cost of the soul-consuming things that are null. knowledge becomes his king, and he will follow it down any path even inside the wilderness they were never meant to walk through. instead of creating they follow everything and anything created. imagination within the patients, which The Light created, bows to what he now believes imagination is. it is a game, and this game in particular makes the soul minute compared to the knowledge that the mind may experience. his time becomes a sacrificed servant, and all each player can do is waste time when they are trapped in this game. he does not realize this game is a war for his soul. what intrigues me most is how one can be drawn against their one soul and the figment of knowledge makes them hate the thing which makes them, them.

A MODERN DAY SCREWTAPE LETTERS

i must humbly confess i have even had my eyes captivated by its *omniscience* nevertheless i recall the mission of tormenting my patient and i will fixate on that fully. i cannot believe the sheer power of this new light. it brings forth addiction with no knowledge of its physical effects. many strive to walk away from addiction when it permeates the flesh because its tactics are easily seen but with this new light the majority of the effects are a war within, so it goes unnoticed. from my knowledge, this new light openly numbs and destroys the patient from the inside out. what is unique about the new light is it is destructive by distraction, so it does not seem lethal to those who do not know what death really is. the new light is a cloud over our patient's mind while it slowly brings one's soul to the grave along with their ceasing flesh. my dear friend, we can sit back and watch as our patients are consumed entirely by whatever darkness the new light *shines*.

> YOUR BELOVED OLDER BROTHER,
>
> *HAVOC*

CHAPTER 5

mirror mirror

dear mr. sagewort,

    we have known for centuries that the identity of a patient controls the entirety of one's being. like never before have we been able to use the body to become the patient's identity. it is as if his body and soul are one instead of soul and spirit. friend, this artifact makes me ecstatic for the latter days to come. i desire to confront the patient with a brute force of overwhelming thoughts. may i tell you a secret? this leaves the patient desolate in thoughts that are not even his own. these thoughts are of the flesh which he is bound to for the time being.

considering these thoughts, i want to teach you about the mirror. it reflects an image of his body back to him. now i know you will ask me why this matters. well, if one is distracted with thoughts that are not his own how will he ever realize what is his own. with the mirror, all he can do is think of thoughts about the body it portrays. he will fall into circular reasoning. *a never ending cycle* where at first the thoughts he has of his body seem ambitious because he can set goals, but darkened thoughts always seem comforting to the flesh. it is a blanket to the heat deprived soul. they shiver and wait for comfort. to a mind wandering in this frigid desert, the temporal fleshly thoughts seem like an all-consuming fire when it is not even a mere flame. keep it that way and your patient will be bedridden in their own flesh, lying there with lack of true comfort. he has desired a comforting touch and love since the day we met him. suffocate him from this and continue to tell him lies about who he is and who he is meant to be. let it take its course like venom in the veins. these thoughts of oneself will come from the inside and burst out.

    if he does not know how to think of himself how will he see the One who created him in himself? infiltrate the mind with darkness of self pity and loathing so that he may not know Light was meant to invade every crevice. he will work nine to five to the business of his body and what he sees it as. all he will know is false accusations and theories of the outer body. he becomes a worker of his body instead of a worker of the field. incapsulating every portion of his mind with thoughts of his body. as time passes, he will cry screeches of agony in hatred of himself. Yes, allow him to hate himself. he will become ill from the hatred. the patient may now believe he is sick not because of internal issues nor even through visible illness to the flesh, but rather through a sequence of thoughts put into the mind to ponder for days, years, or even months. how i see it is The Light is known to come quietly and gently to our patients so why don't we come in as an abrupt blur? a mirror is sharp and gets to the point of what it is trying to show our patient. with that being said, use it to your advantage by being quick to speak into his delicate ear. let me give you an example to further direct you towards using this notion: The Light desires to speak what He calls "Truth" into the patient's heart but if we speak our truth into his heart, he may just very well believe us.

the mirror has become the modern day corset. i desire my patient to look at himself. no no no, i desire my patient to look at *every. single. crevice* of himself so he does not realize how he was made. it will cause him to study portions of himself and speak judgments and accusations into his being. force him to continue to gaze upon himself in the mirror. this will cause him to idolize fixing that broken body of his. the same body that will one day cease to exist. what i love about this mechanism is he looks diligently at his body without seeing every strand of DNA formulated within himself. it enforces a problematic constitution of fallacies in his mind. imagine that you can trick your patient into looking so *closely* at himself that he is not even looking at himself closely at all. the patient becomes blind to the remarkable details of his structure and criticizes the foundational pieces of himself. mirror mirror, an effect ready to be gazed upon by a docile eye.

    i understand why this works so well. it is because he was meant to be a mirror for the Light, reflecting Its aura throughout the earth. fortunately for the weak, it is easier for one to look at the mirror and see himself than it is for him to become a mirror of something greater than himself. little does he know if he worked as a mirror for Light to shine off of him, he would end up seeing himself more clearly. but he doesn't need to know that. perhaps at some point, he may become so consumed by the temporal flesh that he is unaware of the Spirit who created him and made him for eternal glory.

YOUR BELOVED OLDER BROTHER,

HAVOC

CHAPTER 6

a ball of clay

comparative reasoning

dear mr. sagewort,

clay is moldable and forms every which way pressure is placed. when it is mixed with water it is mobile by the hand of whoever holds it. the smallest decision can change its shape for the rest of its existence. weathering and erosion over time make clay vulnerable to weakened structure causing cracks and pieces shipping off. the human heart can be an awful lot like clay. agony and hurt are to the heart like weathering and erosion is to clay. agony and hurt may harden the heart and make it vulnerable to brokenness. trauma is like minerals for a rock's formation. we need to use trauma to harden his heart as he learns and grows. right now, your patient's mind is unstable as he is in his main learning years. he has been confused and hurt by those close to him leaving him desolate in wonder and understanding. i have a fun game we could try because of these conditions. why don't we help him formulate what he thinks of himself? i talked briefly in a prior letter about a thing i like to call comparative reasoning and i would like to further explain it. this is a comparative mindset where every waking thought forms the clay of his heart into whatever lie we may narrate. Love tells him he is seen while i think we should tell him he needs to be seen by more people in more ways.

remember how much he adores his friends? why not
tell him to care about everything they think of him?
he has a very close friend group. others are more
known than him so put thoughts of being less than in
his mind. your patient will never be satisfied if he
spends all the days of his life comparing himself to
others.

he will never have a good enough smile. look.
he will never have the biggest muscles. look.
he will never be the tallest in the room. look.
he will always have too many pimples. look.
the scar on his face will never go away. look.
perhaps if he wasn't so skinny? look.
well now maybe he has too much muscle. look.
get him to look at his mortal body and tell him
comparative mortal thoughts. the mortal body is a

distraction to the beauty and majesty held within the eternal soul. the very soul that is within him. with this method, his thoughts make fragile emotions. comparative reasoning molds the patient by his flesh and by his flesh's imperfections. the flesh is weak so we can craft it into whatever we please. what scares me is if he walks at all by the Spirit that can reside within him. i know many of his arrogant friends do so and he is on the cusp of doing so too. we need him to stay away from these disgustingly pure thoughts. for one who listens to what we tell the flesh will be tossed around by the waves and carried around by every wind of teaching we utter. while if you allow your patient to be consumed by Love he will be sturdy on eternal reasoning and ideologies that do not blow with the wind. his acquaintances are strong, single him out. we need to keep the patient as brittle as a leaf. he must be willing to consume whatever we feed his mind. the only way to do this is to reveal more things to him in hopes of him thinking that fixing that problem will finally be his solution. what many do not realize is you cannot have a temporal solution when their problem is eternal. reward him for the little problems he fixed and give him adoration and praise saying, "well done good and faithful slave". sorry i mean servant. entice him to believe he is serving himself by bettering himself for those around him. at some point, you will no longer have to strive to mold the clay of who he is because he will exhort all his strength in doing it himself. the patient will become molded by his own hands, dead by his own hands, hardened by his own hands, flawed by his own hands, and soon shattered in anger by his very own hands.

>YOUR BELOVED OLDER BROTHER,
>
>*HAVOC*

CHAPTER 7

eternity on earth.

dear sagewort,

the mind is a playground in which we may create any toys and slides the patient desires. like the expanding universe, unending in his eyes, but we know at some point it will all come to an end. nevertheless, if we continue to portray an earth of longevity the presupposition will be that time is on his side. he will spend all the days of his life fixated on what he can gain from this world next. however, how can time be on his side when it is relative? even the existence of time changes. though this is the case if all he thinks is "time is relative". an exemplary place for him to be. as he seeks the universe with everlasting curiosity, he will become like a star shining bright unknowingly waiting for the day it becomes dim. or a flower blossoming in hopes of its day of withering. teach your patient to live to die rather than dying to live. in the past we have brought forth a beautiful construct that seems to continue to work. "you only live once." we know this to be true without telling the patient the entirety of the statement. it is much better stated "you only die once." i urge you to keep your patient away from the knowledge of that though. let him enjoy the brisk air of fall and the summer night drives ending by the fire. if he does not see that life is a gift on borrowed time and that all these things are only a mere moment, then he will hold his life like a time capsule.

he mustn't think of the end unless he fears the end, which i have not seen in this patient yet.

    if this becomes the case, allow him to tremble at the very thought. traversing and quaking in fear to the point that he becomes crippled. the masses allow mystery to invade their thoughts and provoke a new reality of earth and her age. he indeed could fall into this mouse trap as well. he will muster up his own reality and recreate what has already been created into their own. he is not crippled by the thought of eternity. since eternity and death do not scare him, tell him to embrace each moment and hold dearly to every moment instead of asking him to ponder on the things that could come after death. he will love this world and the moments held within it so much he could even forget the end could come at any moment. if he only sees the vastness of this wilderness called life, he will get lost exploring and searching in the depleting world for an eternal reward. he searches for jewels such as diamonds and rubies yet is blind. unknowingly he may pick up moissanite and we may whisper to him that it is the most precious diamond he has ever *seen*. diamonds are like time in the Light. pure, calming, comforting, and glorious. the treasure he looks for is not found in what he seeks. diamonds and jewels are like eternal love. he has forgotten this as we have given him the moissanite. moissanite embodies distraction. use the beautiful things and people around him as distractions as they love him well. love that distracts can become a patient's motivation for life.

the times he laughs with his friends and the time he won the championship with his team. get him to reminisce to the point he becomes ambiguous about his next great goal. if he focuses on these past moments, it will be hard for the Great Reward of eternity to be on his mind. the patient loves this life so much he may never realize or even care to realize there is a far greater eternity that awaits him. at this very moment he seems to be passionate about sustaining the earth and her health without realizing that her, him, and everyone else who enters the playing field of the earth will all be brought back to dust. the dust the earth is becoming is the same dust it came from and is the same dust he came from. for all will blow away in due time. everything has a season, and one day his season on the earth will be no more.

the sun will set one more time. the flowers will bloom for one more spring. the birds will sing one last song. he will breathe his last breath and be ours, forevermore.

YOUR BELOVED OLDER BROTHER,

HAVOC

CHAPTER 8

desires of the heart

dear mr. sagewort,

i urge you to give your patient the desires of his heart. if one fixates on the desires of his heart, he may never be able to see what the soul craves. the temporal satisfactions of the patient's flesh will sustain him long enough to hinder him from filling the eternal emptiness of the soul. this will deplete the patient entirely and is done by observing the patient closely. i have noticed he loves different unique contraptions. the goal is to allow him to desire more and more things from others and the earth. give just him enough to manufacture a desire for even more things. do you see the cycle we can make friend? when he gets one thing it will leave him wanting something else, but a pinch better. it will force our patient to fall into a false *wage dilemma.* to get something new he will then believe he has to work for it. he will fall into deep waters of working for wages which encapsulates him into thinking he must work for everything he desires. if he constantly performs to receive something, a conjunction in his heart will happen with work, money, receiving items, or even better, receiving Love.

    overload him with the desire to work for all he and the ones he loves has. his desires will then become the desire to please himself and those around him. the patient then will not have enough time to think before desiring another contraption because all

he wants now is to make sure everyone and anyone
(including himself) gets what they want. these desires
deafen the ears of his heart from the cries of his soul,
Love, his heart's real desire. the desire for money
will intertwine with a false theory of love he has now
made all by himself. the deafened ear cannot hear
what is needed to feed the crying soul so it will do
anything to make the pain go away; even bring forth
false desires.

      my dear friend, i have some thoughts for
you to ponder as you use this tactic on the patient.
what will dehydrate the soul while making it feel like
it is being quenched? what makes your heart ache?
what is something that can seem everlasting in the
moment but is truly gone with the wind? where is his
gaze and how will you captivate his gaze? tell me,

my friend, what is an extravagant thing that catches your eye. for many of them, it is simple. they are full of greed. give your patient the desires of his heart in a way that makes him rely on these things. if he relies on his desires, he won't be able to rely on the One who implements the true desires of the soul. i say to you once more, it is fairly simple. study him carefully and allow the patient to draw near to particular things until finally there comes a point of obsession. the Light should be his obsession but if the eyes of his heart are on another it is nearly impossible for him to see the Fiery Eyes gazing upon him. those Eyes are always Love filled looking upon the patient. if the patient fixates on his heart rather than allowing the eyes of his heart to guide his desires, he will never see what his heart truly craves. i leave you with this;

draw near to his temporal desires and hone in on the

minute lovers in his life.

> YOUR BELOVED OLDER BROTHER,
>
> *HAVOC*

CHAPTER 9

a cloud of deceit

dear sagewort,

a troubled heart can deceive like clouds on a rainy day. when clouds appear, many forget the sun's entire existence while rain falls on their face and skin. all that becomes known are the hairs that stick up and the goosebumps that cover their bodies. as the cold rain drips on the skin and brings forth a unique smell to the nostril it stimulates the mind from reality. all you hear, feel, see, and think is rain and clouds. the reality of the sun's capabilities is dismantled as the human eye seems to see rain appear from east to west. a misconception by the patients, i say to you even as the clouds cover his view the sun in all its radiance still shines. the sun is a formidable opponent to the clouds. clouds are like a patient's suffering. we must fully consume him in a cloud of deceit, so he does not feel the sun's comforting rays and stays shivering in the gloom-filled murky puddles of agony. all he knows is the weight of the rain on his clothes he does not realize the sun has been trying to keep him warm all along. the suffering of our patient is all he knows. he believes it is all he will ever have and experience, he has no hope of a sunny day. do not let the winds, clouds, or rain stop for even a nanosecond. downpour everything you have on him through words and actions of others, tragedies, and isolation through it all. if we can get him to only see the storms in the world, he will slowly forget the thought that the sun is what sustains life on earth.

the sun furthermore emits heat for the earth in perfect and minute ways. storms are brought forth, yet vegetation still thrives. for that matter, the rain helps sustain the vegetation. it is hard for the patient to grasp this truth when it feels as if the waters from the heavens drown life down below. many wait for one sunny day to withstand all the rainy ones, rather than seeing what we see. that both were meant to grow the patient. suffering and hardship are made to draw the patient closer to the Light but if we use it the correct way, he will feel left desolate in the storm with no shelter. he will perish within his own mourning. a cloud of deceit will be his portion because he will not see rain for what it is made for.

friend i am telling you this to make sure you do not allow him to come to know this. we see this because we are on the exterior of the physical. we can see a dichotomy between the sun and rain. if the patient fixates on the heat of the sun, he will never see the strength in the warmth it provides to bring forth continuation of life. just as if he sees the rain as something that drowns him, he will never see it was made to help him feel the warmth of the sun extensively. use this to your advantage my friend. allow this to be a cloud of deceit over the patient's eyes. if he does not see suffering or pain rightly, he will continue in the ways of a hungry weed instead of a blossoming sunflower. a cloud of deceit is a sin conscious mindset. the cloud of deceit is hopelessness and self-loathing. the patient sees the flaw in all creation instead of seeing the depth of creativity used in all creation. if all his soul sees is a disfigured ideology of what is in front of him, then he cannot grasp the importance of it all. he will see anguish in vanity instead of beauty.

    a cloud of deceit is a blockade for the heart to 1. see the Sun in its full glory and 2. see the Rain as an essential portion to life and life abundantly. your patient can be easily distracted by the things around him. do not let the patient see the Light. we despise the Light. if we can get him to look at a dimmed light, he will never see the Enemy as the full Light He is. put yourself in front of him and prevent him from seeing the Light. sin distorts what the Light portrays. it is like a scratched lens. with the patient, social media is at the forefront of his idolatry. all you have to do is torment him with the dimmed light of his phone and he will never see the pain and agony he's going through. he is beyond distracted. the patient does not see it as torment. when he does see the torment, he blames the Light for the torment instead of the dimmed light that comes from the cloud of deceit. once again i say to you brother you have sculpted into his mind. the thought that rain is against the sun not partnering with the sun. there is balance where he is distraught. in the past, i would strike patients directly with thoughts to show them the weight of torment making them think that it was all from the Light. striking them still works, but i have found this strategy a bit more productive. subjective truths that objectify the One Truth.

how can the patient love the Light if his eyes are on the false light and what the false light shines? the reality is he cannot. so as long as we sustain his relationship with the light produced by his phone, fame, and fortune the heat from the sun will never feel the same on his skin. the phone's light is a substantial way a cloud of deceit if formulated. the truth is, the dim light we are showing him and every other patient in this era, is not Light at all. it is still darkness. when his friends explain the Light to him, he is aggravated. all he has ever seen is the false light we show him. all he has ever seen is a cloud of deceit blinding his eyes from true Light. all he has ever seen is sin and the exorbitant toll it takes on humanity.

a deception of Light, right now, it is the most effective strategy. ninety percent of the tactics

now involve deception. the cloud of deceit will
benefit you as you try new ways to devour and
torture the patient. if the patient truly thinks the
lights, we place in front of him are greater than the
Light that makes us tremble: everything will be okay.
the key to this construct is to sustain the lights in his
face. if not, he will see the empty hole in his soul
because Light will shine in the abyss and reveal it to
him. that is the most dangerous thing that could
happen. once he has seen the dark pit inside of
himself, he will be moved to find out what could
possibly light it up. we both know there is only One
who can do such a thing. so, keep the patient
distracted from this Truth. or, if one finds the
darkness within himself, make sure he thinks the
Light is the one who put the darkness there. in his

eyes Light shall become the ruler of darkness. he will never turn towards Him. he will soon find comfort in the rain and not even desire the sun anymore. he will find comfort in the cloud of deceit we have immersed him in. he will hate true Light and find a light source in everything and anything else. if his eyes burn at the sight of Light he will always think that darkness is better. i present to you the deception of Light. it is a cloud of deceit hazing over his spiritual eyes. he will think his darkness is Light because of the hatred in his heart for the Light. our king is pleased with this type of work.

    i stated this earlier but i would love to go into depth about certain darkness we can portray as Light. my dear friend this is a new era. rejoice! it involves lovers who are deceivers. phones, television, fame, fortune, image, passion, and emotion can all be used to falsely satisfy the patient's soul. our job has become easy. most patients have chosen blindness blatantly. the fog has become the multitude's destiny and they have chosen to deceive themselves. rejoice i tell you! we have very little work to do because the patient is already in the darkness of these falsehoods.

    although this is the case do not be deceived and stay on guard. the Light that met paul surely can meet mere foolish men of today's age. we must hold fast to these ways. keep your guard up. continue tormenting for all the rest of the earth's age. be steadfast in deceit and show the patient how much greater these lesser things are. allow sin to fog what he sees. fog his thinking, his sight, his ways, his emotions, and his being. do not let him see what we see. form a cloud of deceit over his eyes forevermore.

      YOUR BELOVED OLDER BROTHER,

            HAVOC

CHAPTER 10

fear, futile, and future

dear mr. sagewort,

something needs to be addressed in your current tactics. we mustn't continue in the old ways of the fear tactic. perhaps the old ways may have pertained to those prior to this new era but i cannot see it being a subsequent way for the latter days. fear can either cripple the patient or force them to pursue a comforter called fear. fear can be both beneficial and a hindrance for us. i am writing you this letter because of my concerns. if you continue with fear as a strategy, you must be forceful. fear is something that must be brought forth like a crashing wave. fear cannot become a current or the patient will learn to float and overcome his fears. he must drown in his fears. anxiety is meant to cripple a patient to the point of desperation. fear brings forth reliance, it is always a gamble using fear. fear can force the patient to rely on others or worse, to rely on the Light. fear for humans is utter darkness. it is desolation. fear is like being in a desert with no water. it is like being in the arctic with no fire. fear isolates you in deep waters of your own imagination. in my opinion, it is the darkest form of darkness because fear comes from within and is near to the soul. fear is predominantly formulated in the mind. if the patient believes the fear mongering his soul will be silenced from speaking the truth to his mind. fear is the marriage between the mind and the body as the body's aches infiltrate the mind. he was made for unity between the soul and mind because they will be eternally separated from the body. fear must be dealt with carefully because fear can open the mind to the ideology that there has to be something greater to conquer the fear. everything in this world has a conqueror, belittle him with thoughts and defeat him.

      fear is like the darkness of a tavern and fire is like Light that warms the tavern. he mustn't find the fire in his dark and cold tavern. if you use fear as a tactic the patient must end up crawling on the ground, begging us for mercy on his flesh and disregarding the grace to fill his soul. fear must make him desire safety and comfort in his skin that he does not have in the moment. i have loved using fear in the past because it is so fun but i have lost patients because i was not cautious while doing so. i have watched many become fully healed, running into their Home because of my mistakes and i do not want the same to happen to you.

    the patient must stay hurt and not seek the Solution. fear is meant to cause the patient to look for numbing, not healing because numbing is a fast and effective way to diminish what is happening. numbing is like a blanket of hopelessness in the tavern. one can grab this to sustain heat for the time being, but it is ineffective to help one get out of the tavern.

    fear is also like a tornado, when you see it from the outskirts it will terrorize you and demolish every wall you built up. keep destruction in his sight. he has worked hard to be the man he is today.

demoralize his heart and leave him in the dust alone.

fear must become his future. then, and only then, will

he see all things as futile, including his own life. a

dark and cold tavern. desolation will be his portion.

he will be trapped in fear forevermore.

                YOUR BELOVED OLDER BROTHER,

                                  HAVOC

CHAPTER 11

lights against Light

dear mr. sagewort,

it's sickening how bright The Light is. all He does is get in our way and ruin our plans. it deteriorates my heart to see one patient after another run out of our hospital fully healed. we made this place to keep sick patients here forevermore so we mustn't allow more to frolic freely out of this place. i wish there was a way to make those who follow The Light seem like darkness so that those in darkness think they are on a path of Light. invert the roles. make the upside down kingdom upside down because the reality is it was meant to be the right way. if one thinks the path is grand, humongous, and extravagant they will abhor walking on the narrow, beaten, and treacherous path. especially since the masses strive to walk on their own rather than with Light. it is unfortunate how easy it can be for those who have embraced themselves in Light because all they see is Light, so it makes their hearts impenetrable.

      since your patient still walks in darkness there is hope even if some of his friends are in Light. he is sensitive and cares immensely about what they have to say about him even if he does not show it. so, reveal all things they say as darkness. let it be a sword that pierces and wounds him rather than a helping hand of aid and guidance. he will soon become hardened to the words they speak to him. you may ask how we make sure he sustains this lifestyle?

it is quite simple. allow the patient to fixate on the
rugged and mucky path beneath his filthy feet so he
cannot see the Sun shining in front of him striving to
guide him from west to east. if he continues to look at
the beaten path all he will see are the feet of those
walking around him, rather than the Light that
radiates off his friend's faces who have The Light
within them. he sees the dirt between their toes rather
than their clean faces with abrupt smiles. like many
things i have depicted, this is *crucial* for the patient.
he will start seeing all other patient's begrimed feet
rather than their spotless souls that sing in front of his
very eyes. every dark crevice will be focused on
rather than the masterpiece of the canyon as a whole.
how could you love the sunset when your eyes are
fixated solely on a crummy blackened cloud? look at

the view as a whole. the vibrance of the colors have been taken out of view just as the character. the same thing happens if one's mistakes are highlighted more than one's heart. use the little lights words against the patient like the crummy blackened cloud without the sun. his gaze will be on darkness so all he will see others for is *their* darkness.

real love will translate to hate in his heart and hate will translate to love. compassion will be judgment and judgment will be compassion. peace will be anxiety and anxiety will be peace. nothing will be right because the patient will not be able to comprehend what is right and what is wrong. i urge you to speak these things into the listening ears of the patient. tell him the things he is seeing that are darkness are Light and vice versa. if a patient who is now in The Light becomes deceived by our tactics optimize the moment in a timely matter. allow the sick patient to hear the words of the little Lights like a noisy gong continually banging. if he hears their words without love he will not feel the gentle warmth of the Sun Rising through the words. he will feel the crisp and sharp morning winds instead of this warmth. nothing will be right to his wrong viewing mind. haunt him with the speech of those close to him. crucify his heart with their love. allow persecution to plagiarize love in his mind, interpreting it as darkness and hate rather than the gentle care it really is. they are little Lights striving to shine on such a dark soul. they really love him, too bad in his eyes all the love he experiences will appear as hate.

YOUR BELOVED OLDER BROTHER,

HAVOC

CHAPTER 12

what is Love?

dear mr. sagewort,

my dear friend, i am replying to your last letter. to simplify the terminology you used, your question was "what do i tell my patient Love is?" i have an answer for this and it makes me grin to share this with you. i noticed he has been exploring the depths of love with some interest in a friend. prior to anything, i must preface; the love you tell him must fully contradict what Love really is. i noticed you have strived to do just that with this girl you have placed in front of him. my only precaution to this is: make sure she does not allow your patient to subdue

to a fellowship with Light. i see she does follow the
Light closely, so this makes me quiver quite a bit.
couldn't you have chosen another girl? it seems as if
you do not care about our mission whatsoever.
anyways, i have some advice that may entice him, see
the following:

make him see her as his god.

prompt him to desire:

her touch,

her patience,

her kindness,

her voice,

her compassion,

her gentleness,

and whom she is entirely.

A MODERN DAY SCREWTAPE LETTERS

let this lust for her become seductive to the heart and tell him that this is true love. i want him to devote everything to this girl and for him to lay down his life for her. ponder this, but make sure to enforce in his mind that this lust, i mean love, is enthroned forevermore. not for a second shall you allow him to see the lust burning from his heart. i insist you make following the ways of lust pleasurable, which seemingly proposes lust as an axiom of Love. Love is an unending fire that burns from within while lust ever so gently burns in bursts from the outer courts of the body. sometimes so hot it seems as if it is in the inner courts. she loves him and he lusts for her. since this is true, anything can dwindle the flame of love produced by lust. it can be washed away by the sea, blown by storms, shaken by quakes, and frozen by any blizzard to come.

    your job is to then produce a deeper lust around your patient for this girl, and for other things, to make it seem as if he is consumed from within by love. however, we both know he is just surrounded by the lust that sustains this mortal realm. his desire is to care for her. so, allow him to do that with every portion of his life. give him joy and peace when he thinks about her. we have seen how Love is somehow protected even through all the wretched commodities we have used to torment him in this realm so please be cautious. if times become hostile or you are unsure, stir the pot of his heart with rage against her. separation is often beneficial for us to have more time to brainstorm our next move. unfortunately, i am unsure of the immense power Love has and how it is plausible that it can do such great wonders. i do understand how to make lust seem ever so like Love. i know the strength i possess, but i tell you dear friend Love terrifies me. please for the sake of all creation's loss do not allow Love to consume him. continually teach him what love is not. and remember, do not allow her to tell him what true Love is. distract them from having that conversation at ALL costs even if it means you must expose yourself in the midst of them. do not let Love burn inside his heart. keep the temptation of lust close to his mind.

YOUR BELOVED OLDER BROTHER,

HAVOC

CHAPTER 13

work to death

dear mr. sagewort,

    i see he is still with that girl and there seems to be no sight of things worsening. i have an idea on how to ruse him into choosing to submit to our authority and our ways. work him to death. it is peculiar how much he loves her compared to all the rest. he wants to love her with all his heart, all his soul, all his strength, and all his mind so force him to do so. imprint his heart with the perpetual love he has for her. codify his heart to fit the needs of her and her alone. enthrone him into the role of caretaker. she must become his world for him to want to give her the world. without realizing it she will become his golden calf. he will have to strive to sustain this relationship. i wonder if she has started to tell him about the Light. even if she has, he will be so consumed with the work he is putting into the relationship. he won't be able to abide and rest in the Light's ways. this is magnificent because now he will believe he needs to work for her love and once she tells him more about the Light he will think he has to work for His Love as well. all these patients are good for is work. entice him to work harder by giving him affection from her when he does so. twist her words and make it seem like the only way for her to be satisfied is if he gets her more things and does certain things for her. he will run amok after his desire to serve her at all costs as his soul will depreciate from the lack of Love. his life will become work and even she will slip through his fingertips because serving her will leave him empty, searching for more… he will become a robot following every single command you give him. he was meant for day and night worship not workday and night. both seem pleasing to the eye at a moment like this. perhaps this relationship can be permissible after all. for the sake of his soul do not allow it to embark on the journey of Love. allow his every waking moment to be invested in the love of work. he will work on the ship with no acknowledgment of what ship he is on. he will love her "rightly" without knowing what Love is at all.

> YOUR BELOVED OLDER BROTHER,
>
> *HAVOC*

CHAPTER 14

fleeting fame

dear mr. sagewort,

      the desire to be known will turn the hungry into rabid sojourners, devouring anything in sight. you can be known by the masses yet still not known by the One. that is our goal. self deprivation is a necessity for the patient to desire what others want from him. he was meant to only care what his Creator thinks but if he is disillusioned by the opinions of thousands then all he may know is the echoes of the masses. the more voices blabbering his ears off, the less likely he will focus on the Voice calling out to him in his wilderness. just as in prior years the patient longed for others to comfort his sickness, we can allow him to get all the comfort he craves. a poison in disguise as an antidote. little does he know he is just overdosing on the flesh making his mind unaware and numb to the love he actually needs. since the patient loves communal relations, invade his mind with the love of man to the point he is flustered for the rest of his days. he was intended to be in community, but he was not intended for the power of unending community. while community is good for the patient in scenarios such as this, we must use it as a blockade, so he sees it as The Necessity. the patient is meant to worship his Creator but what if we twisted this and introduced the desire to be worshiped? this is what he does when he longs for the affection of his comrades. the patient's mind will turn into a bloodbath of ridicule and unworthiness as he strives to fulfill the depths within. with the new light invented, he can have all the comrades he wants praising him. let the lights of fame flood his eyes. blind him with the lights and deafen him with loud shouts. little does he know people only care about you when you have the blood of others on your sword. the flesh desires to watch you deplete the flesh of another. the flesh is never on their side. all it wants is for the patient to be glorified by the gladiator he can become for it. let him fight for this fame and praise instead of surrendering and bringing fame and praise to the One we know is deserving of it all. one day his body will also deplete, and he will not be able to fight another battle. he will not have another victory. instead, the blood of his flesh will be on the sword of death and the gladiator of fame will sing "death have your sting on this arrogant and pride-filled soldier." watch as he falls to the knees of the one who once gave him all the glory. it is finished. he will be done. the lights will one day burn out and the fame will be no more.

REWIND THE STORY!!!

this is not how we want his story to end. he must be victorious! from gladiator to king of the lands. let the people of his land praise him forevermore. hymns will be sung of him, feasts will be thrown for him, and ceremonies will be placed all for his name. his fleeting name… i mean his famous name… his famous fleeting name. bittersweet ending, right? fame will make him forget that it all comes to an end.

i tell you the *lights will burn out one day, and the fame will be no more.* he will only know himself for the accolades and great victories he had. allow him to reminisce on all *he* has done. a legend to write in all history books. a man who will be known for many moons after his passing while not being written in the most important book… yes, his life will come to an end. the fame may sustain but at least we will be able to deprive him of an eternity of fortune that surpasses his name. he has picked his poison, and he will bring fame to his own name without a single thought of the Name we know is worthy to be praised forevermore. fame is his future and fleeting fame will be his fortune.

YOUR BELOVED OLDER BROTHER,

HAVOC

CHAPTER 15

numb and broken

dear mr. sagewort,

days and years have passed, and he sits in agony for all his life has become. we have hardened his heart through hardships. so far nothing has satisfied his soul. all he knows is darkness perhaps there really is no Light. this world is full of torment, chaos, and pain brought forth by darkness but since "Light" has hurt him it all has to be from darkness. use the hurt. use the very world he proclaims is flawed to numb him from the reality of that brokenness. addiction runs its course like blood in the veins. it becomes as essential for the functioning of the mind just as blood is for bodily life. he has decided to take his hurt and become numb and broken, beaten and bruised.

    this becomes easy because addiction is celebrated in his culture. addiction is agonizing cries of the aching heart turned into an inordinate amount of reliance on erroneous desires. love is comfort to the aching heart through ceaseless adoration, mercy, and grace. it is countercultural to not be addicted. or perhaps it would be countercultural if the patient was addicted to love. guide him to culture. use the brokenness he experiences to force numbness that turns into sufferable addiction. teach him to rely on everything and anything other than the One who satisfies his insatiable heart. every patient was made to rely on something, well Someone and if you observe closely, you will see how no matter who the patient is he or she will use everything and anything to satisfy that inclination. with this patient in particular we have used numerous gadgets to be a reliance for his hands to feel the sense of holding something. the flaw of man brings forth the necessity for a Solution. night displays Day. darkness reveals Light. brokenness proves Healing. addiction shows a patient's need for Incessant Love. in one way or another the patient is numb and broken and must turn to something to mend the broken pot called his heart. with what we have taught him in the past he strives to put the pieces together with his own hand, wisdom, and work ethic. his heart will become more and more shattered the more he attempts to repair it. little does he know every single thing he strives to mend with, besides the One who handcrafted his heart, cannot fix it. only those Hands have the blueprints to fix what deprivation has broken.

why i say numb and broken is because i want you to numb him from knowing he is broken so then he does not know he needs to be put back together through gentle care. in this scenario drugs, alcohol, fortune, and women are a way to numb him from the reality he was made to see. they can become factors of the *cloud of deceit* if used properly. to be clear not all of these things are inherently poor for the patient. with our schemes, we can use anything to numb the body from its brokenness.

he will fall in love with the paralysis because he has not experienced the truth emotions have to offer him. emotions in the eyes of the numb and broken are a hindrance while in the eyes of the healed are a great servant. once again, he has not experienced healing Love so he sees all these things as hate. he is numb to his brokenness so he is also numb to his healing and believes nothing can heal him. a pit he has stuck himself into. he will roll around in the filth of his thoughts asking for a way out without looking for a way out. this has become home. make his pit of brokenness and his comfort in numbness be the sole reason he will never leave.

YOUR BELOVED OLDER BROTHER,

HAVOC

A MODERN DAY SCREWTAPE LETTERS

*freedom is the essence of understanding what
the soul was truly made for.
the flower blooms when it knows its most vibrant
colors will be shown, beaming in all its brilliance.
not a single eye can look away from what it has
become.*

*freedom is the essence of seeing what
the soul is in need of.
the sun stretches in relief only after the darkest
moment of mourning.
the trees wave their branches in celebration
of what they know is to come.*

*freedom is the essence of hearing what
the soul longs for.
freedom is a hymn sung by all of creation.
freedom is from and to and through the Wind that
encourages all to dance along with shouts and
praises.*

A MODERN DAY SCREWTAPE LETTERS

CHAPTER 16

seeing the Light

dear temporal world,

      i am unsure how to start this. i am free, i am finally free. this is what it feels like to have purpose. this is what it feels like to have freedom. i was in a hospital i did not know i did not need to be in. bedridden by drugs given to my mind to deceive me of the pain my soul was going through. today i ran free from that place. no longer will i lie in a bed that i was not meant to die in. i will never listen to the doctor of lies nor will i pay the bills for the debt that has already been covered. i have been healed.

the darkness tormented me for decades and i have gained sight as i run out of this abyss into the most beautiful sunrise i have ever seen. i was shackled down by my own limbs and now i use them to frolic in the field that awaited me all along. for many moons, i pondered the word "Truth" and traveled as a vagabond scavenging all around the earth for clarity. i see it now, the Light has been exposed in my darkest moment. what is this warm feeling in my chest? it is like nothing i have ever felt before. it is as if the sun shines on the dew of the morning heating up every portion of my heart. i tell you i am free and i do not know where to go from here. i must shout it from the rooftops, go to the marketplaces, and tell my friends. i worked so hard to find out that to see all i had to do was close my eyes and let Light see for me.

    if there is no Light there is no sight. for one to see they must acknowledge the truth that all sight is from, through, and for Light. sight can only come from Light for sight is not a thing in darkness. sight comes through Light for Light reflects into the retina sinking deep into the mind. when you experience Light from being in darkness for so long all you see and can now think is Light and the warming comfort of it. finally, my eyes see Light for the Light. i now embark on the journey of telling all of the Light i can now see. it would be foolish of me to tell others of all the darkness i saw when i was blind because i saw nothing but now that i see because of Light i must explain to anyone who will listen what it feels like to see. i am no longer numb and broken nor looking at fleeting fame. see friend, i want to be consumed by Light. the Light is Love. this is Love, it comforts, brings peace, joy, fulfillment, satisfaction, guidance, truth, and Light. Light prevails even on the dark path. those who were meant to show me Light brought me to. the Light restores even that beaten path. i no longer fear but hope in all things. i have full confidence because Light is now who i am, It is my identity. the Light is so bright nothing can deceive me from seeing it clearly. even as i walk through the darkest, coldest, and rainiest days of my life i cannot help but see Light traverse it all. my heart is changed forevermore. i want to spend all the days of my life in the warmth of the Light, held forevermore. please will You never let me go? Light moves my heart in immeasurable ways. i desire the Light to mold me into whatever It wants, oh how i ought to shine in honor of what has happened within. i desire to now be like the Light to all in the darkness guiding others on a path of remolding to their original form and intent. there is only One Light who can shine in the darkest crevasses of the soul, nothing else comes close. my eyes, my body, my mind, and my soul are consumed with Light.

    every desire of darkness has dissipated away and all i care for is what Light reveals to me. close your eyes. No, seriously after you read this sentence my friend i urge you to close your eyes. take a deep breath and breathe out. imagine the brightest object you have ever seen shining on the portions of your heart no one has observed. now watch as the mighty

wave of power of the Light touches your heart ever
so delicately. everything else has crashed on my heart
like a wave but this, this holds my heart with pure
intent and care. close your eyes and watch as the
Light does this very thing to your heart. can you feel
it? an unexplainable freedom.

*before going forth i urge you to take time to close
your eyes and imagine this, i believe it may impact
your heart in indescribable ways *

it is like the first breath on a brisk day or
like the sun touching your skin for the first time in a
while. can you feel the goosebumps form as your
hairs stand up? my body bows at the freedom my
soul experiences. the very essence of the thing that

bound me for so many years must yield to the path of

the Light and where It takes me. i say once more i am

free from the trenches of darkness in my soul and i

see the Light of this world. the Light who shines

within me forevermore.

>   *love,*
>
>   *a former patient of darkness*

A MODERN DAY SCREWTAPE LETTERS

TANNER LAUZON

CHAPTER 17

following the Light

dear mr. sagewort,

    my heart is in anguish, shattered into thousands of pieces. how could you allow him to get away so easily? i gave you an exorbitant number of strategies yet you let foolishness be your portion! he was invested in sin and now he is submerged in a sea of grace. why must i suffer for your wrongdoings? Light is so irritable. scheming like a thief in the night to snatch him out of our hands. the patient was stuck in our trap and somehow, he found the key. the pain and agony i feel as i see those near and dear to my heart become free. how did the Light wiggle through an impenetrable fortress? the poison has drained out of his soul as the Antidote becomes part of his blood. there is no hope for us with this hope filled patient. identity has seeped into his being. the seed has been planted in good soil. the patient was on the verge of everlasting death and now he frolics in the pastures of Life that endure forever. he was in our hospital taking every ounce of the drug of lies and now he is nowhere to be found. it seems as if every good thing always comes to an end.

    there is nothing we can do now but mourn our loss. unless there is a way to continue to torment him as he walks on this new path. this is magnificent! perhaps he does walk in Light now, but we can surely make his path a bit muddy. he will fall and fall and fall we just need to figure out how to trip him. i am unsure of how to do so at the moment but at least this brings hope to my hurting heart. i will get back to you soon, my dear friend. we will conquer this obstacle together. he will be ours and he will tremble at the wrath of darkness.

                YOUR BELOVED OLDER BROTHER,

                              HAVOC

TANNER LAUZON

A MODERN DAY SCREWTAPE LETTERS

CHAPTER 18

a cry for identity

dear patients and sons,

we are all in search. this life is a cry for an eternal identity. this world would be folly if all it was here for was a couple of billion humans to one day perish. there must be something greater and that thing is an Eternal Light that shines in the darkness of a temporal world. we were not made with the ill intent of living temporary lives. friends, we were made for eternal love, grace, and mercy. as our bodies decay and tarnish into dust with the earth our souls explore eternity forevermore. why do you think our flesh desires to be vagabonds of this earth? it is only because our souls were meant to wander forevermore in the love they were created through. the soul was not meant to perish with this faulty body. there must be a deeper root to why all thoughts go against the body and never against one's soul. it is because you were made for so much more. you were made for love and made to love. you were not meant to live for this world or the demons who torment it because that is not living at all, that is just an early access to death. you were meant to serve love by being loved. do not fall into the fallacy of your fleshly truths. they will change and one day strike against you, poisoning you with a venom the enemy created. darkness has been our identities for too long. allow the love Light radiates to be the antidote for all problems. let it alter the entirety of your being. find identity, seek Truth, and do not let darkness consume you all the days of

your life. today Light can and will prevail, shining

through the darkest taverns of your mind and soul.

today you shall see hope.

today you shall see peace.

today you shall see love.

today you shall see Light.

   love,

    a former patient of darkness

CONCLUDING THOUGHTS

the reasoning for this writing is quite simple. i want to bridge the gap between literature, philosophy, and those who abhor these things. i wrote this book, 1. to show what is truly happening at all times and 2. to provide modern context to C.S. Lewis's profound literary work "The Screwtape Letters".

a reminder to whoever just read this book: this book is not meant to imply that things like social media, relationships, fame, money, friends, etc. are bad. rather, it is to show that the devil will stop at nothing to conquer and devour your soul. even if it means using the things closest to you and turning them into idols. he did the same thing with the

Israelites and the golden calf, so why wouldn't he with us?

    for years i was crippled with verbal and physical torment from demons. through that, i learned what they would say, how they would say it, and who they were. once i met Christ i realized why they did these things. i believe it is because there is only One Absolute Truth and His name is Jesus Christ. if truth is subjective then there is no truth at all because it is ever changing. i challenge you to think for yourself. i want you to learn by asking questions. why are we here? how were we created? why are we different than every other species? what is the meaning of life? what is love? who told us all of these things and why do we believe what we believe? personally, i believe heavily in cause-and-effect theory. that everything stems from something and that means there had to be One Source at the beginning. everything else is against that One Source UNLESS it is for that One Source. if we don't have any absolute eternal truth then everything is relative, and relativity leads to chaos.

    i believe so many ideologies have been brought forth over the years but what intrigues me about them all is somehow, someway they either point to God, to love, or our necessity for both. this book is meant to expose everyday lies we may have fallen into. to show that there are things greater than us, for us and against us. whether you believe in God or not, i hope you enjoyed the dialogue that took place and were inspired in some sort of way. lastly, i would like to end with this; no matter who you are, where you come from, what you believe, or how you interpreted all of this.

you are loved.

your dear friend,

tanner lauzon

A MODERN DAY SCREWTAPE LETTERS

TANNER LAUZON